INSTANT POT
RECIPES

*Delicious Recipes for Cooking in a Short Time
with your Pressure Cooker*

BOB LEROY

Table of Contents
Sommario

Introduction

What is an Instant Pot and how do you use it?

Some people have fallen in love with their Instant Pots. They might love blenders, adore their flaming slow cookers, and need a robot in the kitchen, but the Instant Pot is the one they can't live without anymore.

What is an Instant Pot?

It's a small appliance with huge potential, and in the size of a large pot, it packs an electronic pressure cooker, slow cooker, rice cooker, and yogurt maker. Ingenious isn't it?

If you are already the proud owner of a traditional pressure cooker that is now keeping company with a dust colony in the back of the last kitchen cabinet because of the fear you have that it will explode in your hand, I feel like reassuring you immediately. What makes this new generation of digital pressure cookers different are just the safety features, including sensors that keep track of temperature and pressure level.

All you have to do is connect it to electricity and push a button, the instant pot will do it all by itself. It's as simple to use as the slow cooker, only the cooking times are significantly less.

But what does this thing do that's special?

For one, it cooks whole pieces of meat divinely and super fast. After just under 90 minutes, an entire pork shoulder is so tender that it can be cut with a breadstick, and it tastes amazing, too. The same recipe made with a slow cooker takes about 7 hours to achieve the same result and still the meat isn't as juicy and flavorful. The key to being happy with your electric pressure cooker is to choose recipes where you need to get a smooth and juicy result.

What the Instant Pot looks like

It is a large stainless steel pressure cooker with different capacities (and different prices depending on which one you choose), it has a lid and lots of buttons that will help you set the program you prefer, decide the temperature and the time you want it to start cooking. This is in case you want it to prepare dinner when you are not there and find it ready as soon as you cross the threshold of the house. It is easy to wash because inside the appliance there is a removable stainless steel pot, which you can remove and wash and even use on the stove if you miss one. Inside the package, you will also find a steel basket if you want to try steaming. And the instruction booklet. I know we live in an age where it is no longer used to stop and read how to use something, we are all learned, but do it because this thing is very easy to use but not as intuitive. It only takes 5 minutes for the basic functions. Invest this time for the sake of your future dinners. Don't be fooled by the name, because Instant is just that, the name. It's a quick way to prepare recipes that would otherwise take a lot of time and energy to make. But you must calculate the downtime well. Once the pot is closed it must come under pressure, and it will take at least 15 minutes, when it has finished cooking your food it must slowly release the steam safely before opening, and even for this operation count about ten minutes. However, I feel like I can tell you from the results you get, that the game is worth the candle.

How much what the Instant Pot?

The cost depends a lot on which model you want to buy. The basic model has all the features you need to start cooking with an electric pressure stove, the only thing you can't prepare with the basic model is yogurt which is available from the slightly higher model, the Duo. The Duo Plus is the best-selling model of all since it can also prepare cakes, cook eggs and even sterilize food, and it costs twice as much as the basic model. Then some ultra-technological models have buttons to customize the cooking endlessly, Bluetooth, apps, programming complex recipes, and so on. I'm still of the opinion that to start with, the basic model will bring you joy.

But what do I cook in this Instant Pot?

In this pot of wonders, you can cook all the meat you can think of. Especially large cuts, which would take a long time to cook the traditional way. For example, you could try cooking veal with tuna sauce, even trying the low-temperature function. In addition to the old-fashioned way, you could also try your hand at more daring preparations such as veal ravioli with tuna sauce. You will also obtain fantastic results with braised meats, and I recommend trying braised veal in Barolo wine. But if you're not in the mood for meat, you can always use your digital pressure cooker to cook lentils and turn them into a delicious soup as well. You can prepare whole chicken in it, but be sure to remember to use the sauté function. It will be your special tool for cooking meatloaf. You can also prepare potatoes, especially if they are meant to be mashed.

In this book, you have several very appetizing recipes to use with your Instant Pot. Once you gain skill and experience in using this fantastic appliance, you won't be able to do without it. Enjoy!

Chicken

Easy Autumn Chicken Soup

(Ready in about 40 minutes | Servings 6)

Per serving: 245 Calories; 14.6g Fat; 9.8g Carbs; 18.5g Protein; 2.7g Sugars

Ingredients
1 pound chicken thighs
2 carrots, trimmed and chopped
2 parsnips, chopped
1 celery with leaves, chopped1 leek, chopped
2 garlic cloves, minced
6 cups chicken stock, preferably homemade
1 teaspoon dried basil
1/2 teaspoon sea salt
Freshly ground black pepper, to taste
1 tablespoon fresh coriander leaves, chopped

Directions
Simply throw all of the above ingredients into your Instant Pot.
Secure the lid. Choose the "Meat/Stew" mode and High pressure; cook for 35 minutes. Oncecooking is complete, use a quick pressure release; carefully remove the lid.
Serve in individual bowls garnished with garlic croutons. Enjoy

Holiday Chicken Salad

(Ready in about 15 minutes + chilling time | Servings 6)

Per serving: 337 Calories; 23.7g Fat; 3.1g Carbs; 26.4g Protein; 0.9g Sugars

Ingredients

1 ½ pounds chicken breasts

1 cup water

1 fresh or dried rosemary sprig

1 fresh or dried thyme sprig

3 garlic cloves

1/2 teaspoon seasoned salt

1/3 teaspoon black pepper, ground

2 bay leaves

1 teaspoon yellow mustard

1 cup mayonnaise

2 tablespoons sour cream

1 yellow onion, thinly sliced

1 carrot, grated

2 stalks celery, chopped

Directions

Place the chicken, water, rosemary, thyme, garlic, salt, black pepper, and bay leaves in theInstant Pot.

Secure the lid. Choose the "Poultry" setting and cook for 10 minutes under High pressure. Oncecooking is complete, use a natural pressure release; carefully remove the lid.

Remove the chicken breasts from the Instant Pot and allow them to cool.

Slice the chicken breasts into strips; place the chicken in a salad bowl. Add the remainingingredients; stir to combine well. Serve well-chilled

Chèvre Stuffed Turkey Tenderloins

(Ready in about 35 minutes | Servings 4)

Per serving: 475 Calories; 25.4g Fat; 8.2g Carbs; 50g Protein; 2.9g
Sugars

Ingredients
1 tablespoons olive oil
2 shallots, chopped
2 garlic cloves, smashed
1 carrot, chopped
1 parsnip, chopped
2 tablespoons fresh coriander, chopped
Sea salt and freshly ground black pepper, to your liking
1 teaspoon paprika
1 cup dried bread flakes
1/2 teaspoon garlic powder
1/2 teaspoon cumin powder
1/3 teaspoon turmeric powder
2 ½ cups turkey stock, preferably homemade
4 ounces chèvre cheese
2 pounds turkey breast tenderloins

Directions
Press the "Sauté" button to preheat your Instant Pot. Now, heat 1
tablespoon of olive oil andsauté the shallots, garlic, carrot, and parsnip
until they have softened.
Add the coriander, salt, black pepper, paprika, dried bread flakes, garlic
powder, cumin, andturmeric powder; stir to combine well.
Now, slowly and gradually pour in 1/2 cup of turkey stock. Add the
chèvre and mix to combinewell.

Sunday Turkey and Sausage Meatloaf
(Ready in about 25 minutes | Servings 6)

Per serving: 273 Calories; 14.8g Fat; 14.5g Carbs; 22.6g Protein; 4.5g Sugars

Ingredients
3/4 pound ground turkey

1/2 pound cooked beef sausage, crumbled

1/2 cup tortilla chips, crushed

1/2 cup dried bread flakes1 tablespoon oyster sauce

2 eggs

1 onion, chopped

2 garlic cloves, chopped

Salt and ground black pepper, to taste

1 teaspoon cayenne pepper

1 cup tomato puree

3 teaspoons brown sugar

Directions
In a mixing bowl, thoroughly combine the ground turkey, beef sausage, tortilla chips, dried breadflakes, oyster sauce, eggs, onion, and garlic. Season with salt, black pepper, and cayenne pepper; stir until everything is well incorporated.

Add 1 ½ cups of water to the bottom of your Instant Pot. Shape the meat mixture into a log thatwill fit into the steamer rack.

Place the aluminum foil sling on the rack and carefully lower the meatloaf onto the foil. Mix thetomato puree with 3 teaspoons of brown sugar. Spread this mixture over the top of your meatloaf.

Secure the lid and choose the "Manual" mode. Cook at High pressure for 20 minutes or to aninternal temperature of 160 degrees F.

Once cooking is complete, use a natural release and carefully remove the lid. Bon appétit!

Creamed Chicken Cutlets with Herbs

(Ready in about 25 minutes | Servings 6)

Per serving: 422 Calories; 8.5g Fat; 41.5g Carbs; 45.6g Protein; 2g Sugars

Ingredients
1 pounds chicken cutlets
Kosher salt and ground black pepper, to taste
1 teaspoon dried oregano
1 teaspoon dried basil
1 teaspoon dried rosemary
1 teaspoon dried parsley flakes
1/4 cup dry white wine
2 cups vegetable broth
2 garlic cloves, minced
1/2 cup double cream
2 tablespoons cornstarch
6 cups pasta, cooked

Directions
Season the chicken cutlets with salt, black pepper, oregano, basil, rosemary, and parsley. Pressthe "Sauté" button to preheat your Instant Pot. Once hot, cook the seasoned chicken cutlets for 5 minutes, turning once during cooking. Add thewhite wine and scrape the bottom of the pan to deglaze.

Pour in the vegetable broth. Add the garlic and secure the lid.

Choose the "Manual" mode and High pressure; cook for 8 minutes. Once cooking is complete,use a quick release and remove the lid. Reserve the chicken cutlets, keeping them warm.

Stir the double cream and cornstarch into the cooking liquid.

Press the "Sauté" button and simmer for 6 minutes or until the cooking liquid has reduced byhalf. Serve with warm pasta. Bon appétit!

Pork

Family Pork Stew

(Ready in about 15 minutes | Servings 5)

Per serving: 279 Calories; 10.1g Fat; 18.1g Carbs; 30g Protein; 8.2g Sugars

Ingredients
1 teaspoons olive oil
1 pound pork stew meat, cubed
1 cup tomato paste
2 tablespoons fresh cilantro, chopped
2 tablespoons fresh parsley, chopped
1 leek, chopped
1 habanero pepper, deveined and minced
1 teaspoon ginger-garlic paste
1 teaspoon ground cumin
1 teaspoon paprika
Kosher salt and black pepper, to taste
5 cups beef bone broth
1 cup sour cream, for garnish

Directions
Press the "Sauté" button to preheat your Instant Pot; heat the oil. Now, sear the meat until it isdelicately browned.

Add the tomato paste, cilantro, parsley, leek, habanero pepper, ginger-garlic paste, cumin,paprika, salt, black pepper, and broth.

Secure the lid. Choose the "Manual" setting and cook at High pressure for 8 minutes. Oncecooking is complete, use a quick pressure release; carefully remove the lid.

Divide your stew among serving bowls; top each serving with sour cream. Enjoy!

Apple Maple Pulled Pork

(Ready in about 35 minutes | Servings 8)

Per serving: 434 Calories; 25.2g Fat; 13.6g Carbs; 36.1g Protein; 10.5g Sugars

Ingredients
2 ½ pounds pork butt, cut into bite-sized cubes
1/2 cup vegetable broth
1/2 cup barbecue sauce
Sea salt and ground black pepper
1 teaspoon dried oregano
1/2 teaspoon dried basil
1 tablespoon maple syrup
1 red chili pepper, minced
1 cooking apple, cored and diced
1 lemon, sliced

Directions
Add the pork, broth, barbecue sauce, salt, black pepper, oregano, basil, maple syrup, chilipepper, and apple to your Instant Pot.
Secure the lid. Choose the "Soup" setting and cook at High pressure for 30 minutes. Oncecooking is complete, use a natural pressure release; carefully remove the lid.
Shred the pork with two forks. Return it back to the Instant Pot. Serve with lemon slices. Bonappétit!

Pork Chops in White Mushroom Sauce

(Ready in about 30 minutes | Servings 6)

Per serving: 438 Calories; 25.8g Fat; 7.2g Carbs; 42.8g Protein; 2.7g Sugars

Ingredients
1 tablespoons butter
6 pork chops
1 tablespoon Italian seasoning blend
1/2 teaspoon coarse sea salt
1/2 teaspoon cracked black pepper
1 pound white mushrooms, sliced
1 tablespoon fresh coriander, chopped
1 teaspoon dill weed, minced
2 cloves garlic crushed
1/2 cup double cream
1/2 cup cream of onion soup

Directions
Press the "Sauté" button and melt the butter. Once hot, sear the pork chops until golden browned,about 4 minutes per side.
Add the remaining ingredients and gently stir to combine.
Secure the lid. Choose the "Meat/Stew" mode and cook for 20 minutes at High pressure. Oncecooking is complete, use a quick pressure release; carefully remove the lid.
Serve over mashed potatoes. Bon appétit!

Festive Pork Roast with Gravy

(Ready in about 20 minutes | Servings 4)

Per serving: 388 Calories; 22.1g Fat; 6.8g Carbs; 36.7g Protein; 3.7g Sugars

Ingredients
2 tablespoons olive oil
1 pound Boston-style butt, sliced into four pieces
Coarse sea salt and freshly ground black pepper, to taste
1 shallot, sliced
2 cloves garlic, sliced
1 stalk celery, chopped
1 bell pepper, deveined and sliced
1/2 cup apple juice
1/2 cup chicken broth
1 tablespoon stone ground mustard
1 teaspoon basil
1 teaspoon thyme
2 tablespoons plain flour, mixed with
2 tablespoons of cold water

Directions
Press the "Sauté" button and heat the oil. Then, sear the Boston butt until it is golden brown onall sides.
Add the salt, pepper, shallot, garlic, celery, bell pepper, apple juice, chicken broth, mustard,basil, and thyme to the inner pot.
Secure the lid. Choose the "Manual" mode and cook for 15 minutes at High pressure. Once cooking is complete, use a quick pressure release; carefully remove the lid. Remove the meatfrom the cooking liquid.
Add the slurry and press the "Sauté" button one more time. Let it simmer until your sauce hasthickened. Spoon the gravy over the pork and serve. Bon appétit!

Pork Masala Curry

(Ready in about 30 minutes | Servings 3)

Per serving: 436 Calories; 19.8g Fat; 18.3g Carbs; 43.7g Protein; 5.2g Sugars

Ingredients
1 pound pork stew meat, cubed
1/3 cup all-purpose flour
1 tablespoon ghee
2 onions, sliced
1 (1-inch) piece ginger
2 cloves garlic, sliced
2 green cardamoms
1/2 teaspoon ground allspice
1 tablespoon garam masala
1 tablespoon cider vinegar
Salt and black pepper, to taste
1 teaspoon curry powder
1 teaspoon coriander seeds
1/2 teaspoon Fenugreek seeds
2 dried chiles de árbol, chopped
1 cup yogurt

Directions

Toss the pork stew meat with the flour until well coated.

Press the "Sauté" button and melt the ghee. Once hot, cook the pork for 3 to 4 minutes, stirringfrequently to ensure even cooking.

Add the remaining ingredients, except for the yogurt.

Secure the lid. Choose the "Manual" mode and cook for 15 minutes at High pressure. Once cooking is complete, use a natural pressure release for 10 minutes; carefully remove the lid.

Add the yogurt and press the "Sauté" button; let it cook for a few minutes more or untileverything is thoroughly heated. Bon appétit!

Classic Pork Chops and Potatoes

(Ready in about 20 minutes | Servings 4)

Per serving: 484 Calories; 24.3g Fat; 20.2g Carbs; 43.7g Protein; 1.1g Sugars

Ingredients

2 tablespoons lard, at room temperature
4 pork chops
1 cup chicken broth
1 onion, sliced
1 pound potatoes, quartered
Sea salt and ground black pepper, to taste

Directions

Press the "Sauté" button and melt the lard. Once hot, brown the pork chops for 3 minutes perside.
Add the remaining ingredients.
Secure the lid. Choose the "Manual" mode and cook for 10 minutes at High pressure. Oncecooking is complete, use a natural pressure release; carefully remove the lid.
Serve warm.

Beef

Country-Style Rump Steak

(Ready in about 1 hour | Servings 6)

Per serving: 355 Calories; 14.2g Fat; 6.5g Carbs; 50.9g Protein; 1.3g Sugars

Ingredients

Sea salt, to taste

1 teaspoon mixed peppercorns, crushed

1/2 teaspoon marjoram

1/2 teaspoon ginger powder

1/4 cup flour

2 tablespoons olive oil

3 pounds rump steak, trimmed and sliced into small pieces

3 garlic cloves, halved

2 carrots, sliced

1 cup vegetable broth

2 ripe tomatoes, pureed

1/2 teaspoon hot sauce

Directions

In a shallow dish, combine the salt, black peppercorns, marjoram, ginger powder, and flour.Dredge the beef pieces in the seasoned mixture to coat on all sides.

Press the "Sauté" button to preheat your Instant Pot. Heat the oil and brown beef until no longerpink.

Add the remaining ingredients.

Secure the lid. Choose the "Manual" mode and cook for 60 minutes at High pressure. Oncecooking is complete, use a quick pressure release; carefully remove the lid. Bon appétit!

Margarita Glazed Chuck Roast

(Ready in about 1 hour | Servings 6)

Per serving: 348 Calories; 14.9g Fat; 10.3g Carbs; 42.7g Protein; 7.7g Sugars

Ingredients
1 pounds chuck roast
1 cup beef broth
1/4 cup soy sauce
1/4 cup champagne vinegar
Sea salt and ground black pepper, to taste
1/2 teaspoon red pepper flakes
2 cloves garlic, sliced
Margarita Glaze:
1/2 cup tequila
1/4 cup orange juice
1/4 lime juice
2 tablespoons dark brown sugar

Directions
Add the chuck roast, beef broth, soy sauce, champagne vinegar, salt, black pepper, red pepperflakes, and garlic to the inner pot.
Secure the lid. Choose the "Manual" mode and cook for 40 minutes at High pressure. Oncecooking is complete, use a natural pressure release for 10 minutes; carefully remove the lid.
Meanwhile, whisk all ingredients for the margarita glaze. Now, glaze the ribs and place under thebroiler for 5 minutes; then, turn them over and glaze on the other side. Broil an additional 5 minutes.
Cut the chuck roast into slices and serve the remaining glaze on the side as a sauce. Bon appétit!

Chunky Beef Chili

(Ready in about 25 minutes | Servings 4)

Per serving: 393 Calories; 17.4g Fat; 23.6g Carbs; 37.4g Protein; 6.9g Sugars

Ingredients
1 tablespoon olive oil
1 pound ground chuck
1/2 cup leeks, chopped
2 cloves garlic, minced
1 teaspoon dried oregano
1 teaspoon dried basil
1/2 teaspoon cumin powder
1 teaspoon ancho chili powder
Kosher salt and ground black pepper, to taste
1 cup beef stock
1 red chili pepper, minced
2 (15-ounces) cans black beans, drained and rinsed
1 (14-ounce) can tomatoes, diced
4 tablespoon tomato ketchup

Directions
Press the "Sauté" button and heat the oil. Once hot, cook the ground chuck, leeks, and garlicuntil the meat is no longer pink.
Add the remaining ingredients; gently stir to combine.
Secure the lid. Choose the "Manual" mode and cook for 15 minutes at High pressure. Oncecooking is complete, use a quick pressure release; carefully remove the lid.
Serve in individual bowls garnished with green onions if desired. Bon appétit!

Delicious Cheeseburger Quiche

(Ready in about 45 minutes | Servings 4)

Per serving: 465 Calories; 28.2g Fat; 9.4g Carbs; 41.5g Protein; 5.7g Sugars

Ingredients
1 tablespoon olive oil1 pound ground beef

1 onion, chopped

2 cloves garlic, minced

Sea salt and ground black pepper, to taste

1/2 teaspoon basil

1/2 teaspoon thyme

1/2 teaspoon oregano

4 eggs

1/2 cup milk

2 ounces cream cheese, at room temperature

1 cup cheddar cheese, shredded

1 tomato, sliced

Directions
Press the "Sauté" button and heat the olive oil until sizzling. Now, cook the ground beef until nolonger pink. Transfer the browned beef to a lightly greased soufflé dish. Add the onion, garlic, andseasonings.

In a mixing dish, whisk the eggs, milk, and cream cheese. Top with the cheddar cheese. Coverwith a foil.

Place the rack and 1 ½ cups of water inside the Instant Pot. Lower the soufflé dish onto the rack.

Secure the lid. Choose the "Manual" mode and cook for 30 minutes at High pressure. Oncecooking is complete, use a quick pressure release; carefully remove the lid.

Let it rest for 10 minutes before slicing and serving. Garnish with tomatoes and serve. Enjoy!

Beef Stew with Sweet Corn

(Ready in about 30 minutes | Servings 6)

Per serving: 223 Calories; 5.6g Fat; 14.4g Carbs; 28.1g Protein; 3.4g Sugars

Ingredients

1 pounds beef stewing meat, cut into cubes
4 cups bone broth
1/2 cup Pinot Noir
1 yellow onion, chopped
2 bell peppers, chopped
1 red chili pepper, chopped
1/2 pound carrots, chopped
Sea salt and ground black pepper, to taste
1/2 teaspoon mustard powder
1 teaspoon celery seeds
1 cup sweet corn kernels, frozen

Directions

Add all ingredients, except for the sweet corn, to the Instant Pot. Secure the lid. Choose the "Soup" mode and High pressure; cook for 20 minutes. Once cookingis complete, use a quick pressure release; carefully remove the lid.

Stir in the sweet corn kernels and press the "Sauté" button. Let it simmer until thoroughlyheated. Taste, adjust the seasonings and serve. Bon appétit!

Hungarian Marha Pörkölt
(Ready in about 30 minutes | Servings 4)

Per serving: 487 Calories; 19g Fat; 11.3g Carbs; 65g Protein; 2.7g Sugars

Ingredients
1 tablespoon sesame oil
1 ½ pounds beef stewing meat, cut into bite-sized chunks
1 cup scallions, chopped
2 cloves garlic, minced Kosher salt, to taste
1/4 teaspoon freshly ground black pepper, or more to taste
2 carrots, sliced
1 jalapeño pepper, minced
4 cups beef bone broth
1 cup tomato purée
2 sprigs thyme
1 teaspoon dried sage, crushed
2 tablespoons sweet Hungarian paprika
1/2 teaspoon mustard seeds
2 bay leaves
1 cup sour cream

Directions
Press the "Sauté" button to preheat your Instant Pot. Then, heat the sesame oil. Sear the beef for3 to 4 minutes or until it is delicately browned; reserve.
Cook the scallions and garlic in the pan drippings until tender and fragrant. Now, add theremaining ingredients, except for the sour cream. Secure the lid. Choose the "Soup" mode and High pressure; cook for 20 minutes. Once cooking is complete, use a quick pressure release; carefully remove the lid.
Divide your stew among four soup bowls; serve with a dollop of sour cream and enjoy!

Fish and Seafood

Haddock Fillets with Black Beans

(Ready in about 10 minutes | Servings 2)

Per serving: 183 Calories; 4.8g Fat; 1.3g Carbs; 31.8g Protein; 0.8g Sugars

Ingredients
1 cup water
2 haddock fillets
2 teaspoons coconut butter, at room temperature
Salt and ground black pepper, to taste
2 sprigs thyme, chopped
1/4 teaspoon caraway seeds
1/2 teaspoon tarragon
1/2 teaspoon paprika
4 tomato slices
2 tablespoons fresh cilantro, roughly chopped
1 can black beans, drained

Directions
Add 1 cup of water to the bottom of your Instant Pot. Add a steamer insert.

Brush the haddock fillets with coconut butter. Now, season the haddock fillets with salt andpepper.

Place the haddock fillets on top of the steamer insert. Add thyme, caraway seeds, tarragon, andpaprika. Place 2 tomato slices on top of each fillet.

Secure the lid and choose "Manual" setting. Cook for 3 minutes at Low pressure. Once cookingis complete, use a natural release; remove the lid carefully.

Transfer the haddock fillets to serving plates. Scatter chopped cilantro over each fillet and servegarnished with black beans. Bon appétit!

Portuguese-Style Fish Medley

(Ready in about 15 minutes | Servings 4)

Per serving: 342 Calories; 20.8g Fat; 14.7g Carbs; 24.6g Protein; 9.2g Sugars

Ingredients

1 pound fish, mixed pieces for fish soup, cut into bite-sized pieces
1 yellow onion, chopped
1 celery with leaves, chopped
2 carrots, chopped
2 cloves garlic, minced
1 green bell pepper, thinly sliced
2 tablespoons peanut oil
1 ½ cups seafood stock
1/3 cup dry vermouth
2 fresh tomatoes, puréed
1 tablespoon loosely packed saffron threads
Sea salt and ground black pepper, to taste
1 teaspoon Piri Piri
2 bay leaves
1/4 cup fresh cilantro, roughly chopped
1/2 lemon, sliced

Directions

Simply throw all of the above ingredients, except for the cilantro and lemon, into your InstantPot.

Secure the lid and choose the "Manual" setting. Cook for 8 minutes at Low pressure. Oncecooking is complete, use a quick release; carefully remove the lid.

Ladle the medley into individual bowls; serve with fresh cilantro and lemon. Enjoy!

Cod Fish with Potatoes and Goat Cheese

(Ready in about 10 minutes | Servings 4)

Per serving: 390 Calories; 17.6g Fat; 20.8g Carbs; 36.5g Protein; 1.1g Sugars

Ingredients
1 pound baby potatoes
2 tablespoons coconut oil, at room temperature
Sea salt and freshly ground pepper, to taste
1 ½ pounds cod fish fillets
1/2 teaspoon smoked paprika
2 tablespoons fresh Italian parsley, chopped
1/2 teaspoon fresh ginger, grated
2 cloves garlic, minced
1 cup goat cheese, crumbled

Directions
Place the potatoes in the bottom of the inner pot. Add 1 cup of water; then, add coconut oil, saltand pepper. Place the rack over the potatoes. Place the cod fish fillets on the rack. Season the fillets with paprika and parsley.

Secure the lid. Choose the "Steam" mode and cook for 3 minutes at Low pressure. Once cookingis complete, use a quick pressure release; carefully remove the lid.

Remove the salmon and the rack from the inner pot. Continue to cook the potatoes until forktender; add the ginger and garlic and cook for 2 minutes more.

Top with goat cheese and serve. Bon appétit!

Traditional Fish Tacos

(Ready in about 13 minutes | Servings 4)

Per serving: 475 Calories; 23.4g Fat; 40g Carbs; 25.2g Protein; 2.9g Sugars

Ingredients
1 lemon, sliced
2 tablespoons olive oil
1 pound haddock fillets
1/2 teaspoon ground cumin
1/2 teaspoon onion powder
1 teaspoon garlic powder
1/2 teaspoon paprika
Sea salt and freshly ground black pepper, to taste
1 teaspoon dried basil
1 tablespoon ancho chili powder
4 (6-inch) flour tortillas
4 tablespoons mayonnaise
4 tablespoons sour cream
2 tablespoons fresh cilantro, chopped

Directions
Add 1/2 cup of water, 1/2 of lemon slices, and a steamer rack to the bottom of the inner pot. Press the "Sauté" button and heat the olive oil until sizzling. Now, sauté the haddock fillets for 1to 2 minutes per side. Season the fish fillets with all the spices and lower them onto the rack. Secure the lid. Choose the "Steam" mode and cook for 3 minutes at Low pressure. Once cookingis complete, use a quick pressure release; carefully remove the lid. Break the fish fillets into large bite-sized pieces and divide them between the tortillas.
Add the mayonnaise, sour cream and cilantro to each tortilla. Garish with the remaining lemonslices and enjoy!

Tilapia Fillets with Peppers

(Ready in about 10 minutes | Servings 4)

Per serving: 239 Calories; 7.6g Fat; 8.5g Carbs; 35.6g Protein; 1.3g Sugars

Ingredients

1 lemon, sliced

4 (6-ounce) tilapia fillets, skin on

4 teaspoons olive oil

Sea salt and white pepper, to taste

1 tablespoon fresh parsley, chopped

1 tablespoon fresh tarragon, chopped

1 red onion, sliced into rings

2 sweet peppers, julienned

4 tablespoons dry white wine

Directions

Place the lemon slices, 1 cup of water, and a metal trivet in the bottom of the inner pot.

Place 4 large sheets of heavy-duty foil on a flat surface. Divide the ingredients between thesheets of foil.

Bring the ends of the foil together; fold in the sides to seal. Place the fish packets on the trivet.

Secure the lid. Choose the "Steam" mode and cook for 3 minutes at Low pressure. Once cookingis complete, use a quick pressure release; carefully remove the lid. Bon appétit!

Crab Salad Sliders

(Ready in about 10 minutes | Servings 4)

Per serving: 413 Calories; 25g Fat; 28.5g Carbs; 18.5g Protein; 2.1g Sugars

Ingredients

10 ounces crabmeat

4 heaping tablespoons fresh chives, chopped

2 garlic cloves, minced

1/2 cup mayonnaise

1/2 teaspoon hot sauce

1 teaspoon Old Bay seasoning

1/2 cup celery stalk, chopped

1 tablespoon fresh lime juice

8 mini slider rolls

2 cups Iceberg lettuce, torn into pieces

Directions

Add 1 cup of water, metal trivet, and a steamer basket to your Instant Pot.Place the crabmeat in the prepared steamer basket.

Secure the lid. Choose the "Steam" mode and cook for 3 minutes at Low pressure. Once cookingis complete, use a quick pressure release; carefully remove the lid.

Add the chives, garlic, mayo, hot sauce, Old Bay seasoning, celery, and lime juice; stir tocombine well.

Divide the mixture between slider rolls and garnish with lettuce. Serve and enjoy!

Beans – Pasta – Grains

Chicken and Barley Soup

(Ready in about 40 minutes | Servings 6)

Per serving: 379 Calories; 5.9g Fat; 48.8g Carbs; 33.2g Protein; 5.3g Sugars

Ingredients

1 tablespoon butter, melted

1 ½ pounds chicken drumettes

1 onion, chopped

2 parsnips, trimmed and sliced

2 carrots, trimmed and sliced

1 celery stalk, chopped

2 cloves garlic, minced

1/2 teaspoon sea salt

1/3 teaspoon freshly ground black pepper

1/2 cup white wine

6 cups chicken broth, preferably homemade

2 bay leaves

1 1/3 cups barley, pearled

Directions

Press the "Sauté" button to heat up the Instant Pot. Now, melt the butter. Once hot, sear thechicken drumettes on all sides for 3 to 4 minutes. Discard the bones and reserve.

Then, sweat the onion until it is translucent.

Add the parsnips, carrots, and celery; cook an additional 3 minute or until the vegetables havesoftened. After that, stir in garlic and cook an additional 30 seconds.

Add the remaining ingredients and secure the lid. Choose "Soup" setting and cook at Highpressure for 30 minutes.

Once cooking is complete, use a natural release; remove the lid carefully. Add the reservedchicken and stir to combine. Ladle into individual bowls and serve hot.

Spaghetti with Arrabbiata Sauce

(Ready in about 40 minutes | Servings 4)

Per serving: 481 Calories; 29.2g Fat; 44.5g Carbs; 15.8g Protein; 11.5g Sugars

Ingredients
Arrabbiata Sauce:
1 tablespoons olive oil
1 (28-ounce) can tomatoes, with juice
4 garlic cloves, minced
1 tablespoon brown sugar
1 teaspoon dried oregano
1 teaspoon dried basil
Sea salt and ground black pepper, to your liking
1/2 teaspoon cayenne pepper
1/3 cup cooking wine
Pasta:
16 ounces spaghetti
2 cups vegetable stock 10 ounces cream cheese
6 ounces Parmesan cheese, grated

Directions
Put all ingredients for the sauce in the inner pot.
Secure the lid. Choose the "Manual" mode and cook for 10 minutes at High pressure. Oncecooking is complete, use a natural pressure release for 10 minutes; carefully remove the lid.
Stir in the spaghetti and vegetable stock.
Secure the lid. Choose the "Manual" mode and cook for 5 minutes at High pressure. Once cooking is complete, use a natural pressure release for 10 minutes; carefully remove the lid.
Divide your pasta between four serving bowls. Top with cheese and serve. Bon appétit!

Rich Kidney Bean Soup

(Ready in about 25 minutes | Servings 4)

Per serving: 534 Calories; 15.2g Fat; 72.5g Carbs; 31.4g Protein; 5.9g Sugars

Ingredients

6 ounces bacon, cut into small pieces
1 leek, chopped
2 garlic cloves, sliced
1 parsnip, coarsely chopped 1 carrot, coarsely chopped
Sea salt and freshly cracked black pepper, to taste
2 canned chipotle chilis in adobo, chopped
1 teaspoon basil
1/2 teaspoon rosemary
2 cups dried red kidney beans, soaked and rinsed
4 cups chicken broth
A small handful cilantro leaves, roughly chopped

Directions

Press the "Sauté" button to preheat your Instant Pot. Now, cook the bacon until crisp; reserve.Add the leek and garlic; continue to sauté an additional 3 minute or until they are fragrant.
Stir in the other ingredients, except for the fresh cilantro.
Secure the lid. Choose the "Manual" mode and cook for 8 minutes at High pressure. Once cooking is complete, use a natural pressure release for 10 minutes; carefully remove the lid.
Afterwards, purée your soup using a food processor or an immersion blender. Serve garnishedwith fresh cilantro and the reserved bacon.
Bon appétit!

Lima Bean Hot Pot with Bacon

(Ready in about 20 minutes | Servings 4)

Per serving: 493 Calories; 27.7g Fat; 45.6g Carbs; 17.9g Protein; 11.7g Sugars

Ingredients
8 ounces bacon
1 yellow onion, chopped
2 garlic cloves, pressed
1 pound dry lima beans
3 cups chicken broth
3 cups water
1 cup tomato sauce
1 bay leaf
1 sprig rosemary
1 sprig thyme

Directions
Press the "Sauté" button to preheat your Instant Pot. Cook the bacon until crisp; crumble with a fork and reserve.
Add the onion and garlic and continue to cook them in pan drippings until tender and fragrant.Now, stir in the remaining ingredients.
Secure the lid. Choose the "Manual" mode and cook for 12 minutes at High pressure. Oncecooking is complete, use a quick pressure release; carefully remove the lid.
Discard the bay leaf and garnish with the reserved bacon; serve warm.
Bon appétit!

Black Bean Tacos

(Ready in about 35 minutes | Servings 4)

Per serving: 487 Calories; 11.5g Fat; 75.5g Carbs; 23.8g Protein; 8.1g Sugars

Ingredients
1 tablespoons sesame oil
1 onion, chopped
1 teaspoon garlic, minced
1 sweet pepper, seeded and sliced
1 jalapeno pepper, seeded and minced
1 teaspoon ground cumin
1/2 teaspoon ground coriander
16 ounces black beans, rinsed
4 (8-inches), whole wheat tortillas, warmed
1 cup cherry tomatoes, halved
1/2 cup sour cream

Directions
Press the "Sauté" button and heat the oil. Now, cook the onion, garlic, and peppers until tenderand fragrant.
Add the ground cumin, coriander, and beans to the inner pot.
Secure the lid. Choose the "Manual" mode and cook for 20 minutes at High pressure. Oncecooking is complete, use a natural pressure release for 10 minutes; carefully remove the lid.
Serve the bean mixture in the tortillas; garnish with the cherry tomatoes and sour cream. Enjoy!

Rustic Lahsooni Moong Dal

(Ready in about 20 minutes | Servings 4)

Per serving: 235 Calories; 6.3g Fat; 33.8g Carbs; 12.3g Protein; 2.2g
Sugars

Ingredients
Moong Dal:
1 cup moong dal, soaked
2 hours and drained
4 cups water
1 teaspoon curry paste
Kosher salt and red pepper, to taste
1 teaspoon Garam masala
Tarka:
2 tablespoons butter
1/2 teaspoon cumin seeds
3 garlic cloves, pressed
1 white onion, chopped
1 bird eye chili, sliced

Directions
Add the moong dal, water, curry paste, salt, pepper, and Garam masala
to the inner pot.
Secure the lid. Choose the "Manual" mode and cook for 2 minutes at
High pressure. Once cooking is complete, use a natural pressure release
for 10 minutes; carefully remove the lid.
Melt the butter in a nonstick skillet over medium-high heat. Then, sauté
the cumin seeds for 30seconds or until fragrant.
After that, sauté the garlic, onion, and chili pepper for 4 to 5 minutes or
until they have softened.Stir the contents of the skillet into the warm
dal.
Bon appétit!

Low Carb

Apple Pie Granola
(Ready in about 1 hour 35 minutes | Servings 4)

Per serving: 234 Calories; 22.2g Fat; 5.5g Carbs; 2.5g Protein; 5.3g Sugars

Ingredients
1 tablespoons coconut oil
1 teaspoon stevia powder
1 cup coconut, shredded
1/4 cup walnuts, chopped
1 ½ tablespoons sunflower seeds
1 ½ tablespoons pumpkin seeds
1 teaspoon apple pie spice mix
A pinch of salt
1 small apple, sliced

Directions
Place the coconut oil, stevia powder, coconut, walnuts, sunflower seeds, pumpkin seeds, applepie spice mix, and salt in your Instant Pot.
Secure the lid. Choose "Slow Cook" mode and High pressure; cook for 1 hours 30 minutes. Oncecooking is complete, use a quick pressure release; carefully remove the lid.
Spoon into individual bowls, garnish with apples and serve warm. Bon appétit!

Delicious Homemade Burgers

(Ready in about 35 minutes | Servings 4)

Per serving: 410 Calories; 30.1g Fat; 1.4g Carbs; 31.7g Protein; 0.5g Sugars

Ingredients
Keto Buns:

3 tablespoons butter, softened

3 eggs, whisked

1/2 teaspoon sea salt

1/4 teaspoon cayenne pepper

1/2 teaspoon freshly ground black pepper

1 cup almond flour

1 teaspoon baking powder

1/2 teaspoon granulated garlic

1/2 teaspoon onion powder

Burgers:
1/3 pound ground pork

1/2 pound ground beef

Salt and ground black pepper, to taste

2 garlic cloves, minced

1/2 teaspoon cumin powder

Directions

Start by preheating your oven to 420 degrees F.

Beat the butter and eggs until well combined. Add the remaining ingredients for the buns andcontinue to mix until the batter is smooth and uniform.

Divide the batter between muffin molds. Bake for 25 minutes and reserve.

Meanwhile, mix the ingredients for the burgers. Now, shape the mixture into four equal sizedpatties.

Add 1 cup of water and a steamer basket to the Instant Pot. Place the burgers in the steamerbasket.

Secure the lid. Choose "Manual" mode and High pressure; cook for 6 minutes. Once cooking iscomplete, use a quick pressure release; carefully remove the lid.

Assemble your burgers with the prepared buns. Bon appétit!

Canapés with a Twist

(Ready in about 10 minutes | Servings 8)

Per serving: 112 Calories; 5.8g Fat; 1.2g Carbs; 12.8g Protein; 0.7g Sugars

Ingredients
1 pound tuna fillets
1/4 cup mayonnaise, preferably homemade
1/2 teaspoon dried dill
1/2 teaspoon sea salt
1/4 teaspoon ground black pepper, or more to taste
2 cucumbers, sliced

Directions
Prepare your Instant Pot by adding 1 ½ cups of water and steamer basket to the inner pot.Place the tuna fillets in your steamer basket. Secure the lid. Choose "Manual" mode and High pressure; cook for 4 minutes. Once cooking iscomplete, use a quick pressure release; carefully remove the lid. Flake the fish with a fork.
Add the mayonnaise, dill, salt, and black pepper. Divide the mixture among cucumber slices andplace on a serving platter. Enjoy

---

Shirred Eggs with Peppers and Scallions

(Ready in about 10 minutes | Servings 4)

Per serving: 208 Calories; 18.7g Fat; 3.9g Carbs; 6.7g Protein; 2.3g Sugars

Ingredients
4 tablespoons butter, melted
4 tablespoons double cream
4 eggs
4 scallions, chopped
2 red peppers, seeded and chopped
1/2 teaspoon granulated garlic
1/4 teaspoon dill weed
1/4 teaspoon sea salt
1/4 teaspoon freshly ground pepper

Directions
Start by adding 1 cup of water and a metal rack to the Instant Pot.
Grease the bottom and sides of each ramekin with melted butter.
Divide the ingredients amongthe prepared four ramekins.
Lower the ramekins onto the metal rack.
Secure the lid. Choose "Manual" mode and High pressure; cook for 5 minutes. Once cooking iscomplete, use a natural pressure release; carefully remove the lid. Bon appétit!

Vegan

Spicy Veggie and Adzuki Bean Soup
(Ready in about 30 minutes | Servings 4)

Per serving: 474 Calories; 7.6g Fat; 84g Carbs; 20.5g Protein; 7.8g
Sugars

Ingredients
1 tablespoons olive oil
2 onions, chopped
2 carrots chopped
2 parsnips, chopped
1 celery with leaves, chopped
2 Yukon gold potatoes, peeled and diced
2 ripe tomatoes, pureed
12 ounces Adzuki brans, soaked overnight
1 teaspoon cayenne pepper
1 teaspoon dried basil
1/2 teaspoon marjoram
1 teaspoon black garlic powder
1 teaspoon dried chive flakes
A few drops Sriracha
Kosher salt and ground black pepper, to taste
4 cups boiling water

Directions
Press the "Sauté" button to heat up the Instant Pot. Now, heat the
olive oil and sweat the onionsuntil just tender.
Add the other ingredients; stir to combine well. Secure the lid and
choose the "Manual" mode.Cook for 10 minutes at High Pressure.
Once cooking is complete, use a natural release for 15 minutes; remove
the lid carefully.
Ladle into individual serving bowls and eat warm. Bon appétit!

Chinese Soup with Zha Cai

(Ready in about 35 minutes | Servings 4)

Per serving: 177 Calories; 8.8g Fat; 18.5g Carbs; 7.8g Protein; 7.1g Sugars

Ingredients
1 tablespoon toasted sesame oil
1 yellow onion, peeled and chopped
2 garlic cloves, minced
1 teaspoon fresh ginger, peeled and grated
1 jalapeño pepper, minced
1 celery stalk, chopped
2 carrots, chopped
1 teaspoon Five-spice powder
Sea salt, to taste
1/2 teaspoon ground black pepper, to taste
1/2 teaspoon red pepper flakes
1 teaspoon dried parsley flakes
4 cups vegetable broth
2 ripe tomatoes, finely chopped
1 tablespoon soy sauce
1 cup sweet corn kernels, frozen and thawed
1 cup zha cai

Directions

Press the "Sauté" button to preheat your Instant Pot. Once hot, add the oil. Sauté the onion,garlic, ginger and jalapeño pepper for 2 to 3 minutes, stirring occasionally.

Add the remaining ingredients, except for corn and zha cai; stir to combine well.

Secure the lid. Choose the "Bean/Chili" mode and cook for 25 minutes under High pressure.

Once cooking is complete, use a natural release; carefully remove the lid.

After that, add the corn and seal the lid again. Let it sit until heated through. Serve in individualbowls with zha cai on the side. Enjoy!

Thai Rice with Green Peas

(Ready in about 20 minutes | Servings 3)

Per serving: 306 Calories; 16.7g Fat; 42.7g Carbs; 9.1g Protein; 18.2g Sugars

Ingredients
1 cup basmati rice, rinsed
1 ¼ cups water
Kosher salt and white pepper, to taste
2 tablespoons fresh coriander
4 ounces fresh green peas
2 fresh green chilies, chopped
1 garlic clove, pressed
1/2 cup candy onions, chopped
4 whole cloves
1/2 cup creamed coconut
1 tablespoon fresh lime juice

Directions
Combine all of the above ingredients, except for the lime juice, in your Instant Pot.
Secure the lid. Choose the "Manual" mode and High pressure; cook for 2 minutes. Once cookingis complete, use a natural pressure release for 10 minutes; carefully remove the lid.
Serve in individual bowls, drizzled with fresh lime juice. Bon appétit

Spring Green Lentil Salad

(Ready in about 25 minutes | Servings 4)

Per serving: 183 Calories; 13.8g Fat; 13.7g Carbs; 3.5g Protein; 4g
Sugars

Ingredients

3 cups water
1 ½ cups dried French green lentils, rinsed
2 bay leaves
A bunch of spring onions, roughly chopped
2 garlic cloves, minced
2 carrots, shredded
1 green bell pepper, thinly sliced1 red bell pepper, thinly sliced
1/2 cup radishes, thinly sliced
1 cucumber, thinly sliced
1/4 cup extra-virgin olive oil
2 tablespoons balsamic vinegar
1/4 cup fresh basil, snipped
1 teaspoon mixed peppercorns, freshly cracked
Sea salt, to taste

Directions

Place the water, lentils, and bay leaves in your Instant Pot. Secure the
lid. Choose "Soup" function and cook for 20 minutes under High
pressure. Once cooking iscomplete, use a quick release; carefully
remove the lid. Drain the green lentils and discard bay leaves; transfer
to a large salad bowl. Add the spring onions, garlic, carrots, bell
peppers, radishes, cucumber, olive oil, vinegar, andbasil. Season with
crushed peppercorns and sea salt. Toss to combine and place in your
refrigerator until ready to serve. Bon appétit!

Vegetable and Side Dishes

Moong Dal and Green Bean Soup

(Ready in about 45 minutes | Servings 6)

Per serving: 221 Calories; 4.3g Fat; 34.7g Carbs; 12.8g Protein; 2.1g Sugars

Ingredients
1 ½ tablespoons olive oil
2 shallots, chopped
2 garlic cloves, minced
1 teaspoon cilantro, ground
1/2 teaspoon ground allspice
1/2 teaspoon smoked paprika
1 teaspoon celery seeds
1/2 teaspoon fennel seeds
1/2 teaspoon ground cumin
1 ½ cups moong dal
7 cups water
Sea salt and ground black pepper, to your liking
2 cups green beans, fresh

Directions

Press the "Sauté" button to heat up your Instant Pot. Then, heat the olive oil and cook the shallotsuntil just tender. Now, add the garlic and cook 30 to 40 seconds more or until it is aromatic and slightly browned. Stir in all seasonings; cook until aromatic or 2 minutes more, stirring continuously. Add the moong dal and water. Secure the lid. Select the "Manual" mode and cook for 17 minutesunder High pressure. Once cooking is complete, use a natural pressure release for 20 minutes; carefully remove the lid. Season with sea salt and black pepper; add the green beans and secure the lid again. Select the"Manual" mode one more time and cook for 2 minutes under High pressure.

Once cooking is complete, use a quick pressure release; carefully remove the lid. Serveimmediately with garlic croutons. Bon appétit

Warm Cabbage Slaw

(Ready in about 10 minutes | Servings 4)

Per serving: 136 Calories; 8.4g Fat; 14.5g Carbs; 2.8g Protein; 7.6g Sugars

Ingredients
1 tablespoons olive oil
3 cloves garlic, minced
1/2 cup green onions, sliced
1 pound purple cabbage, shredded
2 carrots, cut into sticks
Kosher salt and ground black pepper, to taste
2 tablespoons soy sauce

Directions
Press the "Sauté" button and add the oil. Once hot, cook the garlic and green onions untilsoftened.
Add the cabbage, carrots, salt, and black pepper.
Secure the lid. Choose the "Manual" mode and cook for 4 minutes at High pressure. Oncecooking is complete, use a quick pressure release.
Lastly, add the soy sauce to the cabbage mixture and stir to combine well. Place in a servingbowl and serve immediately

Roasted Herbed Baby Potatoes

(Ready in about 15 minutes | Servings 4)

Per serving: 198 Calories; 7.1g Fat; 30.3g Carbs; 4.1g Protein; 1.3g Sugars

Ingredients
1 ½ pounds baby potatoes, scrubbed
2 garlic cloves, smashed
1/2 cup roasted vegetable broth
1/2 cup water
2 tablespoons olive oil
1/2 teaspoon paprika
1 teaspoon oregano
1 teaspoon basil
1 teaspoon rosemary
1/2 teaspoon sage
Sea salt and ground black pepper, to taste

Directions
Pierce the baby potatoes with a fork; place them in the inner pot along with the garlic, broth, andwater.

Secure the lid. Choose the "Manual" mode and cook for 10 minutes at High pressure. Once cooking is complete, use a quick pressure release; carefully remove the lid. Drain and reserve.

Press the "Sauté" button and heat the olive oil until sizzling. Now, sauté the seasonings for 30seconds, stirring frequently. Throw the reserved potatoes into the inner pot.

Cook until they are browned and crisp on all sides. Serve warm.

Maple-Orange Glazed Root Vegetables

(Ready in about 20 minutes | Servings 5)

Per serving: 131 Calories; 4.9g Fat; 20.8g Carbs; 2.4g Protein; 13.4g Sugars

Ingredients
1 pound carrots
1/2 pound yellow beets
1/2 pound red beets
2 tablespoons cold butter
2 tablespoons orange juice
1 teaspoon orange peel, finely shredded
1 tablespoon maple syrup
Kosher salt and ground black pepper, to taste

Directions
Place 1 cup of water and a steamer basket in your Instant Pot. Place the carrots and beets in thesteamer basket.
Secure the lid. Choose the "Steam" mode and cook for 10 minutes at High pressure. Oncecooking is complete, use a quick pressure release; carefully remove the lid.
Peel the carrots and beets and reserve; slice them into bite-sized pieces.
Press the "Sauté" button and choose the lowest setting. Cut in butter and add the remainingingredients.
Drain the carrots and beets and add them back to the inner pot; let them cook until yourvegetables are nicely coated with the glaze or about 5 minutes. Bon appétit!

Broccoli with Two-Cheese and Chili Dip

(Ready in about 15 minutes | Servings 6)

Per serving: 246 Calories; 14.5g Fat; 13.6g Carbs; 17.1g Protein; 2.8g
Sugars

Ingredients
1 cup water
1 ½ pounds broccoli, broken into florets

For the Sauce:
1 (15-ounces) can of chili
1 cup Ricotta cheese, crumbled
1 ¼ cups Gruyère cheese shredded
1/4 cup salsa

Directions
Add water to the base of your Instant Pot.
Put the broccoli florets into the steaming basket. Transfer the steaming
basket to the Instant Pot.
Secure the lid. Choose the "Manual" mode and High pressure; cook for
3 minutes. Once cookingis complete, use a quick pressure release;
carefully remove the lid.
Now, cook all the sauce ingredients in a sauté pan that is preheated
over medium-low flame.Cook for 7 minutes or until everything is
incorporated.
Serve the steamed broccoli with the sauce on the side. Bon appétit!

Vegetarian Mushroom Stroganoff

(Ready in about 45 minutes | Servings 8)

Per serving: 137 Calories; 3.9g Fat; 23g Carbs; 4.5g Protein; 2.8g Sugars

Ingredients
2 tablespoons olive oil
1 cup shallots, chopped
2 garlic cloves, minced
2 russet potatoes, chopped
1 celery with leaves, chopped
1 bell pepper, seeded and thinly sliced
1 habanero pepper, minced
14 ounces brown mushrooms, thinly sliced
1 cup water
1 cup vegetable stock
Sea salt and ground black pepper, to taste
1/2 teaspoon Hungarian paprika
1/2 teaspoon cayenne pepper
2 bay leaves
1 ripe tomato, seeded and chopped
2 tablespoons corn flour, plus
3 tablespoons of water

Directions

Press the "Sauté" button to heat up the Instant Pot. Then, heat the olive oil and sauté the shallot, garlic, potatoes, and celery until they are softened; add a splash of vegetable stock, if needed. Stir in the mushrooms, water, stock, paprika, cayenne pepper, bay leaves, and tomatoes. Secure the lid. Select the "Meat/Stew" setting; cook for 35 minutes at High pressure. Oncecooking is complete, use a quick pressure release; carefully remove the lid.

Make the slurry by whisking the corn flour with 3 tablespoons of water. Add the slurry back tothe Instant Pot and press the "Sauté" button one more time.

Allow it to cook until the liquid has thickened. Discard the bay leaves and serve warm.

Green Beans with Pancetta

(Ready in about 10 minutes | Servings 4)

Per serving: 177 Calories; 12.1g Fat; 9.9g Carbs; 8.8g Protein; 2.3g Sugars

Ingredients
1 tablespoons sesame oil
2 garlic cloves, pressed
1 yellow onion, chopped
5 ounces pancetta, diced
1 ½ pounds green beans, cut in half
Kosher salt, to taste
1/4 teaspoon ground black pepper
1/2 teaspoon cayenne pepper
1/2 teaspoon dried oregano
1/2 teaspoon dried dill
1 cup water

Directions
Press the "Sauté" button to heat up your Instant Pot. Now, heat the sesame oil and sauté thegarlic and onion until softened and fragrant; set it aside.

After that, stir in the pancetta and continue to cook for a further 4 minutes; crumble with a forkand set it aside.

Add the remaining ingredients; stir to combine.

Secure the lid. Choose the "Manual" mode and Low pressure; cook for 3 minutes. Once cookingis complete, use a quick pressure release; carefully remove the lid.

Serve warm, garnished with the reserved onion/garlic mixture and pancetta. Bon appétit!

Snacks and Appetizers

Appetizer Meatballs with Barbecue Sauce

(Ready in about 15 minutes | Servings 12)

Per serving: 178 Calories; 9.4g Fat; 8.3g Carbs; 15g Protein; 5.1g Sugars

Ingredients
For the Meatballs:
1 pound ground chuck
1/2 pound ground pork
Seasoned salt and ground black pepper, to taste
1 onion, chopped
2 garlic cloves, minced
1 egg, well-beaten
1/2 cup Romano cheese, preferably freshly grated
2/3 cup tortilla chips, crushed
For the Sauce:
1 cup water
1 cup ketchup
1/4 cup apple cider vinegar
6 tablespoons light brown sugar
1/2 teaspoon onion powder
1 teaspoon ground mustard

Directions
Mix all ingredients for the meatballs. Spritz a sauté pan with a nonstick cooking spray. Heat the sauté pan over a medium-high heat. Then, brown the meatballs until they are delicatelybrowned on all sides.
In another mixing dish, thoroughly combine all ingredients for the sauce. Add the sauce to theInstant Pot. Drop the meatballs into the sauce. Secure the lid and choose the "Poultry" function; cook for 5 minutes at High pressure. Oncecooking is complete, use a natural release; carefully remove the lid.Serve on a nice platter with toothpicks.

Polenta Bites with Cheese and Herbs

(Ready in about 20 minutes | Servings 8)

Per serving: 181 Calories; 8.2g Fat; 22.6g Carbs; 4.1g Protein; 2.7g Sugars

Ingredients
1 cup cornmeal
3 cups water
1 cup milk
1 teaspoon kosher salt
1 tablespoon butter
1/2 cup cream cheese
1 tablespoons cilantro, finely chopped
2 tablespoons chives, finely chopped
1 tablespoon thyme
1 teaspoon rosemary
1 teaspoon basil
1/2 cup bread crumbs
2 tablespoons olive oil

Directions
Add the polenta, water, milk. and salt to the inner pot of your Instant Pot. Press the "Sauté"button and bring the mixture to a simmer. Press the "Cancel" button. Secure the lid. Choose the "Manual" mode and cook for 8 minutes at High pressure. Oncecooking is complete, use a quick pressure release; carefully remove the lid. Grease a baking pan with butter. Add the cream cheese and herbs to your polenta. Scoop the hot polenta into the prepared baking pan and refrigerate until firm. Cut into smallsquares. Spread the breadcrumbs on a large plate; coat each side of the polenta squares withbreadcrumbs. Heat the olive oil in a nonstick pan over medium heat; cook the polenta squares approximately 3 minutes per side or until golden brown. Bon appétit!

Double Cheese Burger Dip

(Ready in about 15 minutes | Servings 10)

Per serving: 253 Calories; 17.7g Fat; 4.2g Carbs; 19.3g Protein; 1.6g Sugars

Ingredients
1 tablespoon canola oil
1 pound ground turkey
1 onion, chopped
1 clove garlic, chopped
2 cups ripe tomato purée
1/4 cup vegetable broth
1 tablespoon
Worcestershire sauce
10 ounces Ricotta cheese, crumbled
10 ounces Colby cheese, shredded

Directions
Press the "Sauté" button to preheat your Instant Pot. Once hot, heat the oil.

Then, cook the ground turkey, onion and garlic for 2 to 3 minutes or until the meat is no longerpink. Add the tomato purée, broth, and Worcestershire sauce.

Secure the lid. Choose the "Manual" mode and High pressure; cook for 5 minutes. Once cookingis complete, use a quick pressure release; carefully remove the lid.

Now, stir in the cheese. Stir until everything is well incorporated; serve immediately.

Barbecue Chicken Dip

(Ready in about 10 minutes | Servings 12)

Per serving: 179 Calories; 7.5g Fat; 14.3g Carbs; 12.9g Protein; 10.3g Sugars

Ingredients
1 pound chicken white meat, boneless
1 cup barbecue sauce
1/3 cup water
6 ounces Ricotta cheese
3 ounces blue cheese dressing
1 parsnip, chopped
1/2 teaspoon dried rosemary
1/2 teaspoon cayenne pepper
1/4 teaspoon ground black pepper, or more to taste
Sea salt, to taste

Directions
Place all of the above ingredients in your Instant Pot.
Secure the lid. Choose the "Manual" mode and High pressure; cook for 6 minutes. Once cookingis complete, use a natural pressure release; carefully remove the lid.
Transfer to a nice serving bowl and serve warm or at room temperature. Bon appétit!

Perfect Cocktail Wieners

(Ready in about 10 minutes | Servings 12)

Per serving: 333 Calories; 23.4g Fat; 19.6g Carbs; 10g Protein; 13.2g Sugars

Ingredients
1 (16-ounce) packages little wieners
1/2 (18-ounce) bottle barbeque sauce
1/2 cup ketchup
2 tablespoons honey
1/2 yellow onion, chopped
2 jalapenos, sliced
1 teaspoon garlic powder
1 teaspoon cumin powder
1/2 teaspoon mustard powder

Directions
Add the little wieners, barbecue sauce, ketchup, honey, onion, jalapenos, garlic powder, cumin,and mustard powder to the Instant Pot. Stir to combine well.
Choose "Manual" setting and cook at Low pressure for 2 minutes.
Once cooking is complete, use a natural release; carefully remove the lid. You can thicken thesauce to your desired thickness on the "Sauté" function.
Serve warm with toothpicks. Bon appétit!

Sesame Turnip Greens

(Ready in about 10 minutes | Servings 6)

Per serving: 73 Calories; 4.3g Fat; 7.1g Carbs; 2.6g Protein; 1.2g Sugars

Ingredients
1 tablespoon sesame oil
1 shallot, chopped
2 garlic cloves, minced
1 pound turnip greens, leaves separated
1 cup vegetable broth
Sea salt, to taste
1/2 teaspoon ground black pepper
1 teaspoon red pepper flakes
2 teaspoons
Worcestershire sauce
2 tablespoons sesame seeds, toasted

Directions
Press the "Sauté" button to preheat your Instant Pot. Once hot, heat the sesame oil.
Then, cook the shallot and garlic until they are fragrant and tender. Add the turnip greens, broth,salt, black pepper, red pepper flakes, and Worcestershire sauce.
Secure the lid. Choose the "Manual" mode and High pressure; cook for 3 minutes. Once cookingis complete, use a quick pressure release; carefully remove the lid.
Sprinkle sesame seeds over the top and serve right away!

Fish and Cucumber Bites

(Ready in about 10 minutes + chilling time | Servings 5)

Per serving: 217 Calories; 14.3g Fat; 10g Carbs; 12.7g Protein; 6.1g Sugars

Ingredients
1/2 pound fish fillets
4 medium-sized tomatoes, chopped
1/3 cup Kalamata olives, pitted and chopped
1/2 cup feta cheese, crumbled
1 tablespoon fresh lemon juice
2 cloves garlic, minced
2 tablespoons olive oil
1/2 teaspoon oregano
1/2 teaspoon dried rosemary
Sea salt and freshly ground black pepper, to taste
5 cucumbers

Directions
Add 1 cup of water and a steamer basket to your Instant Pot. Then, place the fish fillets in thesteamer basket.
Secure the lid. Choose the "Steam" mode and cook for 3 minutes under Low pressure. Oncecooking is complete, use a quick release; carefully remove the lid.
Flake the fish with a fork. Now, add the tomatoes, olives, cheese, lemon juice, garlic, olive oil,oregano, rosemary, salt, and black pepper; mix until everything is well combined.
Cut the cucumbers into pieces. Then, make a well in each cucumber using a spoon. Spoon theprepared fish mixture into cucumber pieces. Serve well-chilled and enjoy!

Desserts

Festive Rum Cheesecake

(Ready in about 25 minutes + chilling time | Servings 6)

Per serving: 399 Calories; 23.7g Fat; 36.7g Carbs; 9.9g Protein; 34.6g
Sugars

Ingredients
14 ounces full-fat cream cheese
3 eggs, whisked
1/2 teaspoon vanilla extract
1 teaspoon rum extract
1/2 cup agave syrup
1/4 teaspoon cardamom
1/4 teaspoon ground cinnamon
Butter-Rum Sauce:
1/2 cup granulated sugar
1/2 stick butter
1/2 cup whipping cream
1 tablespoon dark rum
1/3 teaspoon nutmeg

Directions
Add the cream cheese, eggs, vanilla, rum extract, agave syrup,
cardamom, and cinnamon to yourblender or food processor; blend
until everything is well combined. Transfer the batter to a baking pan;
cover with a sheet of foil. Add 1 ½ cups of water and a metal trivet to
the Instant Pot. Lower the pan onto the trivet.
Secure the lid. Choose the "Soup" mode and High pressure; cook for
20 minutes. Once cookingis complete, use a natural pressure release;
carefully remove the lid.
In a sauté pan, melt the sugar with butter over a moderate heat. Add
the whipping cream, rum,and nutmeg.
Drizzle the warm sauce over the cooled cheesecake. Serve and enjoy!

Peach and Raisin Crisp

(Ready in about 25 minutes | Servings 6)

Per serving: 329 Calories; 10g Fat; 56g Carbs; 6.9g Protein; 31g Sugars

Ingredients
6 peaches, pitted and chopped
1/2 teaspoon ground cardamom
1 teaspoon ground cinnamon
1 teaspoon vanilla extract
2 1/3 cup orange juice
3 tablespoons honey
4 tablespoons raisins
4 tablespoons butter
1 cup rolled oats
4 tablespoons all-purpose flour
1/3 cup brown sugar
A pinch of grated nutmeg
A pinch of salt

Directions
Place the peaches on the bottom of the inner pot. Sprinkle with cardamom, cinnamon and vanilla. Top with the orange juice, honey, and raisins.

In a mixing bowl, whisk together the butter, oats, flour, brown sugar, nutmeg, and salt. Drop by aspoonful on top of the peaches.

Secure the lid. Choose the "Manual" mode and cook for 8 minutes at High pressure. Once cooking is complete, use a natural pressure release for 10 minutes; carefully remove the lid. Bonappétit!

Authentic Agua de Jamaica

(Ready in about 20 minutes | Servings 4)

Per serving: 118 Calories; 0.2g Fat; 29.8g Carbs; 0.2g Protein; 28.5g Sugars

Ingredients
4 cups water
1/2 cup dried hibiscus flowers
1/2 cup brown sugar
1/2 teaspoon fresh ginger, peeled and minced
2 tablespoons lime juice

Directions
Combine all ingredients, except for the lime juice, in the inner pot of your Instant Pot.
Secure the lid. Choose the "Manual" mode and cook for 5 minutes at High pressure. Once cooking is complete, use a natural pressure release for 10 minutes; carefully remove the lid.
Stir in the lime juice and serve well chilled.

Puerto Rican Pudding (Budin)

(Ready in about 1 hour | Servings 8)

Per serving: 377 Calories; 18.4g Fat; 41.7g Carbs; 10.1g Protein; 24.5g Sugars

Ingredients
1 pound Puerto Rican sweet bread, torn into pieces
1 cup water
1 teaspoon cinnamon powder
1/2 teaspoon ground cloves
1 teaspoon vanilla essence
1 cup brown sugar
4 cups coconut milk
2 tablespoons rum
4 eggs, beaten
A pinch of salt
1/2 stick butter, melted

Directions
Place 1 cup of water and a metal trivet in the inner pot of your Instant Pot. Place the pieces ofsweet bread in a lightly greased casserole dish. Now, mix the remaining ingredients; stir to combine well and pour the mixture over the pieces ofsweet bread. Let it stand for 20 minutes, pressing down with a wide spatula until the bread is covered.
Secure the lid. Choose the "Manual" mode and cook for 25 minutes at High pressure. Once cooking is complete, use a natural pressure release for 10 minutes; carefully remove the lid. Bonappétit!

Mini Coconut Cream Cakes

(Ready in about 15 minutes | Servings 4)

Per serving: 425 Calories; 33.6g Fat; 20.2g Carbs; 11.4g Protein; 16.7g Sugars

Ingredients

12 ounces cream cheese
2 ounces sour cream
1/3 cup coconut sugar
1/2 teaspoon vanilla extract
1/2 teaspoon coconut extract
1 teaspoon orange zest
1/2 cup coconut flakes
2 eggs
4 tablespoons orange curd

Directions

Start by adding 1 ½ cups of water and a metal trivet to the bottom of the Instant Pot.

In a mixing bowl, combine the cream cheese, sour cream, coconut sugar, vanilla, coconut extract,and orange zest.

Now, add the coconut flakes and eggs; whisk until everything is well combined.

Divide the batter between four jars. Top with orange curd. Lower the jars onto the trivet. Now,cover your jars with foil.

Secure the lid. Choose the "Manual" and cook at High pressure for 9 minutes. Once cooking iscomplete, use a natural pressure release; carefully remove the lid.

Garnish with fruits if desired. Bon appétit!

Delicious Stewed Fruit

(Ready in about 15 minutes | Servings 6)

Per serving: 193 Calories; 0.4g Fat; 48.8g Carbs; 1.1g Protein; 44.5g Sugars

Ingredients

1/2 pound blueberries

1/2 pound blackberries

1/2 pound mango, pitted and diced

1 cup Muscovado sugar

1 cinnamon stick

1 vanilla pod

1 teaspoon whole cloves

2 tablespoons orange juice

1 teaspoon orange zest

Directions

Add all of the above ingredients to your Instant Pot.

Secure the lid. Choose the "Manual" mode and cook for 7 minutes under High pressure. Oncecooking is complete, use a natural pressure release; carefully remove the lid.

Transfer to a nice serving bowl; serve with frozen yogurt or shortcake. Bon appétit!

Lava Dulce de Leche Cake

(Ready in about 20 minutes | Servings 6)

Per serving: 301 Calories; 15.4g Fat; 32.5g Carbs; 7.7g Protein; 26.1g Sugars

Ingredients
A nonstick cooking spray
1 tablespoon granulated sugar
1/4 cup butter, melted
3 eggs, beaten
1 teaspoon vanilla extract
1/2 teaspoon pure almond extract
1/4 teaspoon star anise, ground
1/4 teaspoon ground cinnamon
1/3 cup powdered sugar
3/4 cup canned dulce de leche
4 tablespoons all-purpose flour
1/8 teaspoon kosher salt

Directions
Spritz a cake pan with a nonstick cooking spray. Then, sprinkle the bottom of your pan withgranulated sugar.

Beat the butter with eggs, vanilla, almond extract, star anise, and ground cinnamon. Add thepowdered sugar, canned dulce de leche, flour, and salt. Mix until a thick batter is achieved.

Scrape the batter into the prepared cake pan.

Place 1 cup of water and a metal trivet in the Instant Pot. Place the cake pan on the trivet.

Secure the lid. Choose the "Manual" mode and cook for 10 minutes under High pressure. Oncecooking is complete, use a quick pressure release; carefully remove the lid. Serve hot with ice cream.

CPSIA information can be obtained
at www.ICGtesting.com
Printed in the USA
BVHW062312140621
609528BV00011B/1670